The Adventures of a
Deaf Tri-Paw

Tammy Pusateri Puckrin

Illustrations by
19th Designs

Disclaimer: This writing is a work of truth and stories that were discussed with the author by professionals who cared for her dog prior to the dog joining the author's family. In many cases, names and places have been changed to names that reflect love and gratitude for a family member, either canine or human, who is important in the life of the author.

Foreword © 2024 by G. Wayne Mello

Copyright © 2024 by Tammy Pusateri Puckrin

Cover, illustrations, and text design © 2024 by 19th Designs

All rights reserved. No part of this publication may be reproduced, distributed, or transmitted in any form or by any means, including photocopying, recording, or other electronic or mechanical methods, without the prior written permission of the publisher, except in the case of brief quotations embodied in critical reviews and certain other noncommercial uses permitted by copyright law.

For permission requests, write to the publisher at the address below.

Tammy Pusateri Puckrin

608 Bell Ave

Sandusky, Ohio, 44870

OR

Visit our website at pusateripublications.com

Library of Congress Cataloging-in-Publication Data

The Adventures of a Deaf Tri-Paw

Tammy Pusateri Puckrin

ISBN: 979-8-9909175-0-7

Printed in the United States of America

Dedicated to...

My Parents,

Tom and Trudy,

who instilled in me a love

for all of God's creatures, and

a sincere desire to help all

animals have a better life.

Foreword

The essence of feeling loved and the longing for inclusion constitutes a fundamental human need, embodying notions of safety, security, acceptance, and peace. It encapsulates the concept of family and belonging. While typically these sentiments are instilled from birth, nurtured, and perpetuated through generations, there exist situations where this isn't always the reality...

Life's fairness and kindness are not guaranteed; it often proves to be harsh and unforgiving. Growing up and navigating existence devoid of comfort and support presents formidable challenges, challenges that do not discriminate based on one's humanity.

Across the vast expanse of the animal kingdom, profound familial bonds prevail. Whether among orcas, elephants, monkeys, or lions, intricate social structures underscore relationships and foster a sense of communal belonging. This phenomenon has long captivated human curiosity. While humanity often perceives itself as possessing unparalleled power, at its core lies something more primal and uncomplicated: love's essence.

The question arises: How can animals harbor such sentiments? After all, they are merely creatures of instinct. Yet, upon closer examination, we discover invaluable lessons to be gleaned from our animal counterparts.

The age-old adage "write what you know" resonates deeply, especially when it comes to tapping into raw emotions. These emotions become accessible when one realizes that everyone, at some juncture, experiences them. Pairing such emotions with a protagonist, particularly one portrayed as an

endearing animal like a mouse or dog, fosters a recognizable and relatable connection.

As you immerse yourself in the story, you can't help but establish a bond with the humble dog, so minuscule amidst the vast expanse of the world. Inevitably, thoughts of your own beloved pet arise, prompting reflections like, "I couldn't bear the thought of my dog being left abandoned, alone and without a family.

Animal stories stand as an enduring genre, weaving narratives that effortlessly capture our hearts. Themes of overcoming obstacles, particularly the quest for belonging, resonate deeply within us, for they echo elements intrinsic to our own nature. "The Adventures of a Deaf Tri-Paw" deftly plucks at these heartstrings, prompting a poignant reflection on the significance of our own familial bonds.

As we witness the struggles and triumphs of the protagonist, we find ourselves cheering for the underdog, rooting for them as they navigate their path to finding acceptance in the world. In doing so, the story serves as a poignant reminder of the fundamental values of family and love, often overlooked or taken for granted by many.

G. Wayne Mello | Author/Illustrator

Maggie Dewdrop series

Acknowledgements

I always read the acknowledgment page in books, and I pray you do as well. I call it the "shout-out" page for a reason, and that is because each of the individuals I am about to mention deserves recognition, tons of love, and all my thanks. Without them, I would not have the courage to even begin to *think* I could draft a book.

God, you are my rock and my mainstay, and it truly is You who deserves all the kudos in my life. Mom and Daddy have had the pleasure of living with my shenanigans for countless years, and I am so grateful for my amazing parents. My handsome husband, Steve, who is as quiet and calm as I am loud and sarcastic, just shakes his head and realizes that being married to an Italian who talks with her hands and is very excitable means his life is never dull. Our three spectacular children, Alyssa, Grant, and Teresa are my greatest blessings and have shown me what it means to be REAL. Then there are Nikki and Paula, my two beautiful sisters from another Mr. and Mrs. who have had my back since first grade; I wouldn't be half the person I am without their constant friendship. My Mr. Sir (Colin) is the little guy I have cared for and loved like my own for many wonderful years and he has my heart and brings me such joy with his smile and hugs. Danny, my soon-to-be newest son, has decided to join our crazy family and loves us despite our weirdness.

Then there are my furriest children, my loving babies that know me better than anyone else and are my confidants. (In case you were wondering, yes, I am one of *those people* who waves at every dog I see!) To my puppers who live in Heaven: Gertie, Toby, Salvadore, Wilbur, Olivia, Rosie (the guinea pig,) and Virginia, and the four doggos who are here in our home (Frances, Carmella, Ernie, and Gennie,) and the pups who are yet to come, thank you for giving me the gift of being your mom and showing me that there is always a reason that dog is God spelled backwards.

Finally, to you dear reader, thank YOU very much! I hope you will see that faith and perseverance help in the darkest of times. Gennie Marie and I are keeping you in our prayers.

Chapters

THE PLACE OF DIRT	11
THE RESCUE	17
SALVADORE'S ANIMAL HOSPITAL	23
ANOTHER TRIP	33
THE DREAM	41
SUNSHINE'S SANCTUARY	45
CONFUSED AND AFRAID	51
MEETING MOLLY	59
VISITORS	67
WILL THEY COME BACK?	75
FINALLY…A FAMILY TO CALL MY OWN	81
HOME	87
MY NEW LIFE AND MY NEW COUSIN	95
THE DREADED PAW-DICURE AND A TRIP TO THE STORE	103
LEARNING HOW TO BE PART OF A FAMILY	113

<u>The Place of Dirt</u>

    Once upon a dog in a land down south, there was a sad and lonely place. Dirt stretched in every direction, and it became a muddy mess when it rained. One large rickety house with peeling paint and broken windows stood next to a barn with a partially missing roof. There were no gardens or flowers, and not a shade tree anywhere. Many dogs (too many to count) lived without shelter in The Place of Dirt, with food thrown on the ground once a day and metal bowls that held dirty water in them only when it rained. There were big dogs and small dogs, puppies, and adults, and some of them looked like one another with light-colored fur that had many darker spots. Since I was a dog, I really couldn't see colors very well, but I could tell that my fur was a bit peculiar because it was almost totally light-colored, and my dark spots were practically invisible. Many female dogs continuously had litters of puppies and tried to protect them from the awful people who never let us inside and kept us tied up in the wind, rain, heat, or cold. This was the place where I was born, and I knew that one of these female dogs was my mom because she tried extra-hard to protect me and keep me safe.

My mom was very smart, and she somehow knew that my ears didn't work like her other puppies. They were in the right place, just like every other pup, but no sound came into them and that is why mom needed to keep me safe from the humans that she taught me could not be trusted. Lots of big equipment was always moving around The Place of Dirt and I couldn't hear it coming or going. This is why I always stayed right by mom and slept next to her side in all types of weather. We were a team, and tried to stay out of the sight of the humans who were never nice to any of the dogs.

One day, I was suddenly taken away from mom, and I was so scared! I could see her trying to get back to me, but the mean people just dragged her away with a heavy chain. What would I do now and where had she gone? I loved her and we needed each other! I would not be able to get milk from her if she wasn't close by and I was now all alone in the world.

Even though the nasty people did not bring out food for the dogs often, when they did, they would just throw it on the ground. Since my ears didn't work, I couldn't hear the food when it hit the bare earth. However, I knew that even if I did see it, it would be too late because everyone else would already have eaten it all. I began to eat small stones and dirt just to not be hungry all the time.

The other dogs were so mean to me, and I just didn't know why, but I tried to stay away from them because I was afraid when they would snarl or try to shove me out of the way. I thought they didn't like me because my ears didn't work like theirs did and that was why they weren't my friends. I decided that if I tried harder to find my mom, I wouldn't feel so hungry. I wasn't going to give up my search because I could still faintly smell her scent, although it was getting harder and harder for my nose to search her out and that is what worried me most.

I knew that I had been looking for my mom for many weeks because I could feel the seasons change and I had lost her scent completely. I became incredibly sad because I realized that she might never be able to come back. Since I couldn't hear and mom wasn't there to help protect me, I hid in the darkest shadows and stayed away from the big equipment that was always moving about at The Place of Dirt.

On one extremely windy day, I felt some vibrations come through the ground and into my body. Suddenly, I saw a large tractor heading right at me and even though I tried to move quickly, the person driving was going too fast and seemed like he wanted to run me over. The horrible man's angry eyes looked right into my frightened face. He had to STOP...but he didn't, and he ran over my right front leg and kept on going! OUCH!!! I was screaming in pain, and even though I couldn't hear myself, I thought that someone would come to help, but not one of the nasty people at The Place of Dirt came; they simply looked the other way.

After this happened, my leg hurt very much, and I couldn't walk on it at all. I had no way to get food or look for mom, so I drank out of muddy puddles that were close by where I laid on the hard ground. I ate dirt and stones as I tried to drag my front leg along, but I could not get far and would just fall whenever I tried to walk. I was sad and hungry and so lonely. If only I was with mom again, she would certainly help! The days went from cold to extremely hot and the sun baked the ground and made it crack. There were no muddy puddles, no shelter, and no way to find food. I wasn't even strong enough to lift my head to look for stones to chew. I became thinner, and my leg hurt more as each minute passed. I knew I was getting extremely sick.

The Rescue

One day not long after the tractor hurt my leg, I saw many vans and lots of people running around. I realized that the vans could hurt me just like the tractor had, and that these people could also be heartless just like the man who ran over my leg! I had to hide, but I realized I could no longer move at all. I felt very warm, and I was dizzy. Worse yet, my leg smelled awful. I didn't even care if I ate dirt or stones or found a muddy water puddle to drink from anymore. I couldn't find my mom, I was hurting, and I just wanted to sleep. I was not even able to hide from the people and vans so I just hoped they would not see me as they ran around with big crates and blankets. What did they need all that stuff for anyhow?

I couldn't hear them coming, but when I opened my eyes and saw them, I growled and barked and showed my teeth. They were smiling at me and saying words, but they didn't know that my ears wouldn't work. I thought that they would be mean to me like the other dogs and people were since my mom wasn't around to protect me anymore. Where was she anyhow? Could these people help me find her somehow? NO! I knew better than to trust anyone! I decided I would bark louder and make my hair stand up on my back; that would make them afraid, and they would go away. I mustered all my remaining strength to make them leave me alone, but the strange thing was, they didn't leave. I was so tired, and I began to fall asleep because my front leg hurt more with each passing minute. Couldn't they see I was hurt? What did they want from me anyway?

    I woke up again and the people were STILL there, but wait a minute…what was that scent? It smelled like some sort of food, and NOT dirt or stones! The people were even smiling and holding some soft little toys out to me, and I thought that that meant they wanted me to take the toys. I eyed them and growled, but softer this time. The people sat down and waited for something; were they waiting for me for some reason? I quickly noticed that I didn't see any dogs running around anymore. Instead, the people with the vans were holding some of the pups and others were being put in crates. They were being nice to the dogs and giving them blankets and food and toys! Was my mom with these people? Would they take me to her somehow?

Just then, the people began to slowly move closer to me and I decided to keep growling, but not as much because one nice lady tossed me one of the soft toys. I sniffed it and this made the people really happy! Then, wonder of all wonders, the nice lady tossed me something that tasted so much better than stones and dirt! It wasn't my mom's milk, but it was yummy! I chewed it up and realized it tasted like some of the meat that I would smell when the people in the ramshackle house would cook outside over a crackling fire. I could eat this all day long!

The people kept smiling and they kept waiting. Before I knew it, they were giving me more meat and I let them get closer and closer until they wrapped me in a blanket. Oh no, what were they going to do with me now? I was so scared of being wrapped up and my leg hurt so much that I barked fiercely, but I could not hear myself. However, the people just kept giving me little bites of food as the nice lady and her friends carried me to the waiting vans. As we got closer, I tried extra hard to sniff out my mom, but I realized that she was truly gone because I could not smell her scent anywhere. I was so sad, but as the nice lady and her friends held me and gave me even more pieces of meat, I grew very tired and knew that I needed to rest. There were so many dogs in the vans, but I could not hear them because my ears were not like theirs, so I slept as the van began to drive away from The Place of Dirt.

After an extremely long time, I suddenly felt the van stop. The people let all the other dogs out to run around, but I couldn't run; I wasn't even able to walk or stand. I slowly looked up and saw the nice lady again. It was then that I realized that I could do something called "reading." I looked at her shirt and there were letters there that spelled "Trudy." I realized that Trudy must be my friend and that mom must have sent her to help me with my leg. She used her mouth to say words to her friends that I could not hear. When her mouth moved, her friends came over to help lift me onto the ground so I could use the bathroom. I looked around and saw leafy green trees and tall grass; I had never seen anything like it before! There were families with children and other dogs that were playing together. They did not look mean. Were they just like my new friend Trudy?

After I was carried back to the van and placed on my blanket with my new toy, I started to whimper because I was feeling sicker, and my leg was sending piercing pains throughout my whole body. The last thing I remembered before I fell asleep was Trudy trying to hold me, but I howled in pain. She looked at me with a heart full of love like my mom used to, and I closed my eyes and prayed for help.

Salvadore's Animal Hospital

Many hours later, I awoke from my nap and found that it was no longer daylight. I saw bright lights shining down through the van windows, and when the doors opened, there were people running out with a bed on wheels. Everyone was moving extremely fast! I looked above the people and read some words that lit up the front of a building called Salvadore's Animal Hospital.

Before I knew it, I saw Trudy's mouth moving as she looked at all the new people. They were not smiling, their faces were heartbroken and worried, like my mom looked when they dragged her away from me and I was so sad. Why were they fearful when they looked at my leg and why were they hurrying? Everyone kept shaking their heads and had tears streaming down their faces. Trudy kissed my head and had tears in her eyes as she walked away. Where was she going?

I felt something prick my front left "good" leg, and I became very sleepy. A mask was placed over my face and air began flowing into my nose. I closed my eyes, dreamed of my mom, and wished I could take her to the place of grass and trees with Trudy, and we could be together again.

When my groggy eyes began to open, Trudy and her friends with the vans, as well as all the other dogs from The Place of Dirt, were gone! Where was everyone? My eyes were so heavy, and I couldn't help but to close them again. I felt so sick that I just kept sleeping fitfully and crying in pain.

The next time I awakened, I saw a man looking at me and I practiced my reading again. His shirt said "Tommy." Tommy's eyes looked genuinely concerned as he made his mouth move, but he didn't know that I couldn't hear what he said. I could feel he was worried, so I became very scared and started to shake. I tried to get up and stand but Tommy motioned to his friends, and they came over and moved me around on a blanket. I looked for my sore leg, but I had a large cone around my head and neck for some reason. I could feel a big bandage on my leg and back. "That is weird," I thought, "my leg must be getting fixed inside that big band aid." Tommy's mouth moved some more, and he smiled as he adjusted the hoses that were coming out of something that was stuck in my left front leg. I figured that if I took a little nap, my leg would show itself after I woke up and Tommy took off my bandage. I fell back asleep dreaming of mom and thinking that I would want her to meet Trudy and Tommy.

As soon as I finished napping, I felt hungry and was wondering if I should begin looking for dirt and stones or a muddy puddle where I could get a drink. I tried to stand, and the lights on a machine began to go off as Tommy and his friends ran over. For some reason, they did not want me to stand, but they did bring me a little bowl of CLEAR water. I had never lapped up anything that tasted so good since I had mom's milk at The Place of Dirt. They did not let me drink much but sat with me and made their mouths move. They even brought over a shiny object that had a tag on it that I read; it said "bell." I wasn't sure why, but Tommy hid the bell behind me, and I could not see it anymore. Then he sat in front of me and shook it back and forth for a while. Why was he acting so strangely with this bell? Did he want me to play with it like the soft toy? It did not seem fun, and I did not give it my attention.

Tommy moved his mouth open and closed again and a new person came over. Then they both moved their mouths and looked at me while Tommy patted my head. They flipped buttons on my machines with the hoses that were stuck in my left front leg and looked at me to see what I would do. I just sat there. Someone moved alongside me and made their hands open and close together repeatedly. I just looked at Tommy. They brought another dog over to stand behind me and I could feel his breath coming out of his mouth as it opened and closed so I knew he must have been barking, but I did not turn to look at this new friend.

Tommy shook his head and hung a sign up next to me; he seemed depressed, just like I had been since my mom had been taken away. Maybe if he knew I could read, he would be happy again. I read the sign that said, "Deaf female, rescued from a puppy mill in the south by Rosie's Rescue, driven through the night up north, right shoulder and leg amputee, spayed, shots, fearful." Hmmm... I didn't know what any of this meant, but I was still proud that I could read.

After another nap, my belly started rumbling so I knew that it was time to get up and search for food. Tommy wasn't watching me too closely, so I tried to stand. I was shocked when I fell right over! What was happening? Why couldn't I stand? Tommy was quickly by my side, and he patted my head and side as he helped me get back on my blanket. I didn't know what to think, but Tommy brought over my soft toy, and even a very tiny piece of what I had learned was meat. He would only let me have a small piece and must have been keeping the rest for himself! I would try to sniff out his pockets if only I could stand, but my leg needed to rest longer under the big band aid. Tommy opened and closed his mouth over and over, and his smile began to make me feel that I could look to him for help in getting back to my mom. He shut off all the lights in the place called Salvadore's Animal Hospital and everyone else left, but not Tommy. He pulled up a chair next to my rolling bed and put his head next to mine and his hand over my chest. Soon we were both asleep.

I woke up the next morning and the place where my bandage was on my body really started to hurt. I thought that maybe if I bit the bandage a little to loosen it that I could get my right leg out and then I wouldn't hurt so much. This seemed like a good plan, but as soon as Tommy saw me biting at it, he came over and put this huge monstrosity around my neck. Didn't he know that if I could just get my leg out, I wouldn't be in pain? How could I do that now? I was getting sadder and sadder, and I could never trust Tommy now. I looked over to see if there was anything new to read and that was when I saw a different sign next to me that said, "Deaf female bandage removal today." I wasn't sure what all that meant, but I DID KNOW that I had a bandage, so maybe it was me and I would get to see my leg again and it would be better. That was something to be happy about because maybe then I could stand and get back to mom.

Before long, Tommy came over with a long-handled object that opened and closed; I read the label that spelled out "scissors." He kept the huge, round monstrosity around my neck so I could not see anything, and he used the scissors to cut my bandage. I could feel him moving the bandage as it started to come off my body. He seemed to take a long time doing this and even put a cool, strong-smelling liquid on my skin. I didn't know what he was doing, but I could tell there wasn't any hair on my skin where he was putting the cool liquid. I figured this might be the last thing needed to make my leg better.

Tommy moved his mouth up and down as he looked across the room and soon another friend came over. They were both moving their mouths and I saw Tommy look up to the ceiling and fold his hands before he and his friend held me in place and took off the huge neck monstrosity. It felt good to stretch and I wanted to tell Tommy that they could let go and I would walk around on my own to go look for some more of that clear water and the little pieces of meat. As I stretched, I looked back and was shocked; my right leg and shoulder were GONE, MISSING, SOMEONE HAD TAKEN THEM AWAY!

I began to tremble, and Tommy and his friend had to hurriedly put the mask with the cool air on my face. I started whimpering and they brought over my soft toy and blanket and laid me down quickly. Many other friends came over and patted my head or smiled at me with encouragement. I didn't understand. When Trudy and her friends with the vans brought me here, I had my leg in the same place it had been. When I went to sleep after being poked in my left leg, my right leg had been there, and when I woke up, I thought it was under the bandage. Wait. A. Minute. I had gone to sleep, and someone stole it while I was sleeping! Could Tommy have let the mean people from The Place of Dirt come in and take my leg? I looked around to see if there was another sign to read that would tell where my leg was located. Nothing.

I looked at Tommy in a pleading way, but he just shook his head and kept patting my side where my right leg and shoulder USED to be before I felt the poke that made me sleep. They even brought me the nice clear water, but I wouldn't drink it and I rolled over and closed my eyes and wished with all my heart that my mom was here to help me find my leg. That night, when the lights were turned off and Tommy brought his chair over and laid his head next to mine, I didn't roll over and look at him, and I fell asleep praying to find my leg.

<u>Another Trip</u>

The next day I woke up and saw a new sign that read, "Deaf Female Tri-Paw to be transferred to Sunshine's Sanctuary today." Who and what was a deaf female tri-paw and where was this sanctuary? I was so tired from being in pain all night and I felt bad that I wasn't being nice to Tommy, so I didn't give the sign much thought. I decided that I would let Tommy help me stand and try to walk, even though I still wondered if he knew where I could find my leg. He came over and gave me a big hug and helped me into a standing position on my three legs. I kept looking for my leg, and when I couldn't see it anywhere, I figured I would walk with Tommy's help, and we would find it together. Walking proved harder than I thought, and I almost fell many times, but Tommy was there to help, and he and I even walked around outside Salvadore's Animal Hospital.

We sat near a bench under a tree so I could rest, and he took his two hands and made them into the shape of a heart as he looked at me and a tear rolled down his cheek. I put my head in his lap and tried to make him feel better. I smelled something coming from his pocket and immediately knew it was the pieces of meat! He smiled and took out each piece and gave it to me; I hoped he would be my friend forever because I sure could use a friend. I was hoping that he might even have enough meat to share with mom when we found her again.

As Tommy and I were sitting outside under the shade tree, a van pulled up and I practiced my reading again. The words on the van said, "Animal Transport: Saving Dogs One Paw at a Time." My eyes grew bigger, and I had hope in my heart! Saving paws must mean THIS van was hiding my leg and Tommy brought me to it so we could find my lost leg together!

A tall man got out of the van and smiled at Tommy; he came over to us and the men shook hands. The new man had letters on his shirt that spelled out "Wilbur." He and Tommy were moving their mouths and smiling at each other. Then Tommy put his hand on my head in a loving way and knelt next to me and smiled through his tears. When a nice person smiled, weren't they happy? Why were there sad tears and a happy smile on Tommy's face? Wilbur didn't seem to notice any of this and began to open the back of his van and look inside. "THIS WAS IT; WILBUR WAS GETTING OUT MY LOST LEG," I thought. I knew just the thing that I could try to do to make Tommy stop crying and have Wilbur see that he could give me my leg back; I would stand without help.

I tried, and it was CHALLENGING work. I was more tired than I realized, and it must have been because I had not eaten enough of the tiny pieces of meat that were hiding in Tommy's pocket! Tommy motioned with his hand to Wilbur, and he ran over, but I didn't want their help; I could do it because I knew it would make them happy. I tried again, but I was too tired and sore, and I just couldn't stand by myself. Why did the place where my leg used to be hurt so much when the leg wasn't there anymore? I wanted Tommy to be happy, but I still needed help to stand and walk. I began to wonder why Wilbur's van would keep my lost leg hidden inside. Couldn't he just get it out and bring it back? THEN I would be able to stand and walk just fine; I might even run!

We walked around the bench under the shade tree for a while, Tommy and Wilbur helping me, and I smelled many spots where other dogs had been. I could tell from their scent if they were happy or sad, sick, or healthy. I figured that dogs would want to know that I had been by this shady spot, so I left my scent behind. It was no easy task for me to keep walking, but Tommy and Wilbur took turns holding onto a long, thick string that was attached to me somehow. It didn't hurt, it just kept me close by so they could help me try to move. I frequently stopped to rest, and they would smile at me, letting me know it was okay. Of course, my plan was to still go find my leg (which I was sure was in Wilbur's van), but if that meant I had to rest and walk a little at a time, I would be patient and show Tommy and Wilbur that I knew how to be the best dog.

After a few nibbles of the small pieces of meat that Tommy thought he was hiding from me in his pocket, we started to walk closer to the van. I was even more certain my lost leg must be in there or else I would not have read the words, "Animal Transport: Saving Dogs One Paw at a Time" on the side of Wilbur's van. I found that it was different walking on grass and then walking on warm, flat pavement. Before coming to Salvadore's Animal Hospital, I had only lived at The Place of Dirt, and only walked on dirt, or sometimes mud if it rained. I had never seen or touched anything else with my paws, (except when we stopped along the road in Trudy's van on the way from The Place of Dirt.)

As the three of us walked closer to the van, I could sense Tommy getting sad again. Didn't he think I was walking well without my right front leg? Wilbur put his arm around Tommy's shoulder and their mouths opened and closed over and over. Tommy kept nodding his head as if he understood why Wilbur was moving his mouth. I decided I better sit down if they were going to just keep opening and closing their mouths. Plus, if I sat down on the ground exactly right, I could hold my head up high and look inside the doors of the van for my lost leg. The funny thing was, I only saw big crates, blankets, and soft toys, just like Trudy had in her vans.

I felt Tommy put his arms around my neck and he looked right into my eyes. I knew that look, it was love, and I had seen it before when my mom looked at me not so long ago before the mean people took her away. I wanted Tommy to know that I loved him too, and even though he was not my mom, I realized he had tried to protect me just like she had done. I whimpered a little, and I told him I loved him inside my heart. I could tell that he heard the way I was able to communicate, because he made that heart shape with his hands again.

Wilbur shook hands with Tommy one last time, and they both picked me up and laid me on a soft blanket in Wilbur's van, right inside a big crate.

I did not like the crate, and I looked at Tommy for help! I could see in his eyes that he wanted me to not be sad or afraid, but it was hard to be brave inside the van that smelled like dogs, and not just any dogs, dogs who were scared! Surely, Wilbur and Tommy did not want dogs to be scared! Tommy hugged me one last time and then he and Wilbur shut the doors. "Wait," I yelped, "don't go!" Tommy backed away, but I could still see him outside the window. Wilbur opened the door in the front of the van, and I felt the vibrations of something underneath me as we started to move! This couldn't be right; I was supposed to be with Tommy! Now I didn't know what to do and Wilbur was driving us so far away that I could only see Tommy waving from a distance. I couldn't stand very well in the crate without help because my leg had not been returned yet, so I sat down and whimpered. What was I going to do now and why did I have to keep going in vans?

    I looked out the window and saw water as we went over a road that was high in the sky and I read a sign that said, "Sentinel Bridge." I knew in my heart that this was okay because my mom had taught me that the word sentinel means to protect, and that is what she, Trudy, and Tommy had done for me until I could not see them anymore. Was Wilbur going to protect me now?

    I settled in and found that the blanket Wilbur gave me was soft and cozy; I had never had anything like this in The Place of Dirt! I even found my soft toy that Tommy had put inside the crate, and I used it as a pillow. I was going to look for my lost leg, but the vibrations that I felt coming from under the van made me sleepy, so I closed my eyes and dreamed about mom. I was sure she was missing me as much as I missed her and if we were together again, we could be a team and look for my lost leg.

The Dream

As I slept, I dreamt of my mom. I saw that she was trying to tell me something. She knew my ears didn't work like other dogs' ears, but she and I always understood each other because we loved one another. It was like I could *feel* what she was saying instead of hearing the words. She was telling me she could not be with me anymore and that I must be brave. My heart started to beat faster, and I was trying to tell her no, she couldn't leave me forever! I was sad and scared; we needed each other, but in my dream, she was getting farther and farther away from me and was going towards a glowing light in the sky. I was trying to run to her, but I could not get up because of my lost leg! Why wouldn't she wait? I could see a Man reach out to scoop her up in His arms as He held her and smiled. Her heart shone brightly with love for me as the Man waved and smiled. In my dream, my ears started to work like other dogs, and I could hear the Man, whom I now recognized as God.

"Sweet pup," God said to me, "your mom no longer lives at The Place of Dirt and will have all the meaty treats and soft toys she wants in Heaven. She and I love you and will be watching over you until it is your turn to come to Heaven." I wanted to know why I couldn't go to Heaven right now! God had just said that He loved me, even though my ears were broken, and I had somehow lost my leg while I was asleep at Salvadore's Animal Hospital.

God must have been able to hear my thoughts because He smiled at me and looked at my mom knowingly. "You are an inquisitive and persevering little pup, just like your mom. It is her time to be with Me now, but you have more to do in the world. I promise you that she and I will both be waiting for you, many years from now, when you come to Heaven." I was confused and looked at mom and God, not knowing what to do.

God sat my mom down, and in my dream, she came to me and gave me a kiss as she nuzzled her head lovingly into my neck. I began to cry as she turned back to God and He told me, "Your mom and I have a family ready for you, but they do not even know it yet. Their hearts are ready for you, and they will learn about you very soon. The mom in this family has been picked by Me for you and she will care for you and love you just like I do because she and her family know that you are perfect in every way." I wanted to ask how I would find my leg without mom's help and how I would know who this family was anyhow, but just then, Wilbur's van rolled over something bumpy, and I woke up. Wilbur's mouth was opening and closing, but I could not hear him like I heard God's words in my dream.

Sunshine's Sanctuary

Wilbur pointed to a sign, and I used my reading skills to find out that it said, "Sunshine's Sanctuary." Wait a second here! I thought I had read something about this when I was still with Tommy. What did that sign say again? I had to think hard because I was still confused from my dream about mom going to Heaven with God. Thinking, thinking...yes, I remembered now; it said, "Deaf Female Tri-paw to be moved to Sunshine's Sanctuary today." STOP! Was I a deaf female? Was I a tri-paw? I looked back and, sure enough, my leg was STILL gone, but I DID have three other legs attached in the right places. My ears seemed to only work when I was dreaming, so that must mean I was the deaf female tri-paw!

Who would want me now? God had told me about a special family, but surely this family would pick other dogs with working ears and all their legs before they would choose me to live with them in their home! Would Wilbur at least help me find my leg? What would I do now that we were at this new place? Sure enough, Wilbur opened the door, and I just knew that I was going to have to be somewhere new again. Wilbur sat down next to me and smiled my way as he started to move his mouth, but my ears were once again proving that they did not work when I wasn't dreaming. I was sad and frustrated. Why were people taking me to unusual places? Why couldn't I hear and why did my leg have to go away? Wilbur patted my head and I just whimpered and looked away. He knew I was sad, and he hugged me as we just sat in the van with the doors open so I could sniff the fresh air.

As I began to look around, I saw two people approaching the van. I tried to see if Trudy and Tommy were with them, but they were gone. I began to growl because I didn't want new people getting close to me and I was determined to just stay with Wilbur. Too much was changing, and I was afraid. The place where my leg used to be began to hurt more and I became overwhelmed with fear. I now was able to tell that the people coming my way were ladies and I let them know I didn't want to meet anyone else. They heard me growl and stayed back so I could sit next to Wilbur. "Good," I thought, "they will leave me alone!" Hoping they would go away, I closed my eyes and pretended to sleep.

When I opened my eyes, I noticed that the ladies were standing closer to Wilbur, and they were all making their mouths do the open and shut movements that I now realized meant they were talking to each other. I was so sad that I didn't even care if my ears worked because I wasn't interested in what they said. I began to growl again, but then I suddenly sniffed something special. I knew that scent; one of these ladies must have gotten meat from my friend Tommy and she had it right in her hand for me to try! She slowly placed her hand flat under my chin and I gobbled the piece of meat up quickly. Wow, it was tasty! I looked up at Wilbur and these people who must be his friends, and they were all smiling. If it made them happy to see me eat meat, they could feel free to share some more anytime! However, they just looked at me and seemed as though they were expecting something.

What could I do to get more meat? Tommy seemed to like to walk me around; was that what these people wanted? I was trying to figure out how to walk out of the van on my own when Wilbur snuck me a piece of the tasty treat and slipped the long, thick string around my neck. Wilbur was trying to help me move, but I was afraid to jump out of the van, so he lifted me like I was as light as a feather.

He gently sat me on the ground, and I tried to stand. It was extremely challenging work and the place where my leg used to be began to throb. I wanted to give up, but then I remembered my dream where God and my mom told me that I was special. I stood for a very brief time and the ladies took out their phones and smiled at me, making all kinds of funny movements, and talking motions that they *knew* I could not hear. I looked at them and Wilbur smiled as they all seemed extremely excited to have their phones pointing at me to take pictures for some unknown reason. This made me very tired, and I sat down to rest because I knew if I didn't, I would fall over.

Wilbur came over, and I knew the look in his eyes because it was just like Tommy's face had been earlier that morning when he was smiling and had tears in his eyes. Wilbur was getting ready to leave me here with these ladies. Was the new family God had told me about at Sunshine's Sanctuary? Would I get my leg back if I went inside the building? It was too much to think over and I snuggled closer to Wilbur and whimpered because I was so sad and had been to so many places since Trudy and her friends came in the vans and had taken me from The Place of Dirt. Everyone I knew left me and even my own leg had gone somewhere without me; it was too much!

Wilbur gave me the biggest hug and kiss and then took his hands and made the heart shape so I would know that he loved me very much. What I didn't get was how people supposedly loved me, and they still left! As Wilbur handed the ladies the long, thick string that was around my neck, I looked up at them and tried to stand, but I was too tired. When Wilbur's van pulled away, I sat in the grass and howled. A new place, and new people again. No one seemed to want to stay with a deaf tri-paw for too long.

The only good thing was that I could still smell the tasty treats that must be hiding in the ladies' pockets. Why couldn't people leave the treats where I could get them and have a snack?!? Maybe if I sat up and wagged my tail, they would give me the tasty meat. With significant effort, I sat up by myself as they both smiled and did indeed give me two little bites to eat. They seemed proud of me for doing this all alone and were doing the talking that I couldn't hear. Then, they both did something I did understand. They each made the heart shapes with their hands and showed me love by patting my head. I wondered if these ladies were my new family. Once again, they had letters for me to read on their shirts; one spelled out "Virginia" and the other spelled "Olivia." They weren't in any hurry to go inside the building and just sat next to me quietly. They didn't try to make me move around but were content to be next to me as I rested.

Confused and Afraid

    I slept without dreaming for a little while, but I woke up when I could smell yummy treats right under my nose. I chewed them quickly and looked ahead as I saw Virginia placing pieces of the meat in an exceedingly lengthy line that led to the building. Olivia was holding onto the long, thick string that was around my neck and tried to help me stand. Did they want me to walk to get the little bites of meat? There sure was a lot of it, and I was hungry! It tasted so much better than the dirt and stones I used to have to eat when mom and I lived with all the other dogs at The Place of Dirt. I wanted to eat more of it, but I was so afraid to walk without all my legs.

    Olivia must have known I was afraid because she placed her body next to mine and Virginia came back and stood on my other side. I took one tiny step and got to eat a treat. Should I try again? Virginia and Olivia were still on each side of me to make sure that I did not fall. I tried again and I did it; one step and one treat. Wow! The building where the treats led to was a little closer now and I could feel the excitement in the belly rubs that my new friends were giving me as they stayed by my side. I devoured another treat, and another, and another! I could not believe it; I was standing right outside the door, and I had walked there with the help of my new friends. Olivia looked at me hesitantly and let go of the long, thick string. Virginia held the door open, and I WALKED RIGHT IN BY MYSELF! How did that happen? Didn't all dogs need four legs to move around? Was I able to walk with just three legs?

Once we were inside, I saw lots of other people and countless cats and dogs. This was different! These animals seemed like they were loved because people were holding them and giving them toys and kisses. Olivia and Virginia seemed to be "my people" and they stayed with me and wrote on various papers. I read a sign that said "Paws-itively Cute Pet Photos Taken Here." Olivia helped me stand near the sign and Virginia took out her phone again and pointed it at me as she snapped photos. Why did they need photos anyhow? I was getting very tired, and I knew it was time for me to lay down because I could see out the window that the sun was setting lower in the sky. Maybe I would just look for my leg tomorrow and try to sleep in this new place tonight.

Olivia and Virginia must have been able to tell I was hurting, because they both walked on either side of me again. We walked past a room with many cats and down a hallway to a room filled with crates and blankets. There were dogs of all sizes and shapes inside these crates, and I could smell that some of them were afraid and lonely. Olivia opened one of the crate doors and Virginia helped me inside. Why was I staying in this crate if these new ladies were supposed to be my family? Shouldn't I be where they were? I laid down on the blanket and waited for them to sit next to me like Tommy had done at Salvadore's Animal Hospital. Instead, they turned around and shut the door! "STOP, DON'T LEAVE ME HERE," I barked.

Where were they going? They walked right out of the room! I began to howl and whimper, "Help me," I was trying to say, "I am afraid to be alone in this dark, new place!" Sadly, I realized that it didn't matter, as nothing brought them back and I was in the big room with the other dogs, but we were each in our own crates. I snuggled into the soft blanket they had left on the floor and prayed for someone to come, but no one did.

I must have fallen asleep because I woke when slices of light began to shine into the room through the windows. Since it was morning, I hoped that meant people would get me out of here. Sure enough, in walked Virginia and Olivia. They smiled and waved at me. Even though I was mad that they left me during the night, I made my tail wag a little. They pointed to my tail, thrilled to see it move!

There it was again, the scent of the good meat bits that I loved! They handed me a piece through my crate and then walked around with more meat for the other dogs. All the dogs seemed happy and ready to play. Olivia walked around filling bowls with fresh, clear water. This was amazing to me because I had only seen clear water when Tommy gave it to me, and I knew it would taste better than the muddy water I used to try and find in puddles at The Place of Dirt. Surprisingly, I saw Virginia start to fill bowls as well, but not with water. What was this stuff? I used my nose to tell me it was like the bites of meat, but a bit different. I was trying to wait for my turn and sat down since I saw the other dogs do the same thing. Olivia and Virginia liked it when I sat and came right over and smiled and made the heart sign with their hands. Wonder of all wonders, LOTS of pieces of what smelled like some sort of food was poured into my very own bowl!

What was this place that gave each dog their own food and no one had to fight for it or scrounge to eat dirt and stones like I used to do when I was with my mom? These bowls of food and water were mine, but I did not know if they would take them away from me, and I thought I better eat and drink it all at once. When Virginia and Olivia saw what I was trying to do, they picked up the bowls and put their hands out flat in front of me and used their talking that I could not hear.

Did they want me to sit again? I tried that, but no, they did not give me back the food and water. I wasn't sure what they wanted, but I still sat there and then they sat down with me in my crate. I decided to keep sitting in case they wanted to be my friends. After we did this for what seemed like a long time, and I saw that they weren't going to eat the food or drink the water themselves, they let me eat and drink some more. I began to understand that they just wanted me to take my time eating and drinking and that they would make sure I had enough to eat. Did that mean they were my family?

I finished and they put the long, thick string loosely around my neck and stood on either side of me as we walked down the hall again and went outside. Olivia walked away from my side and stood out in front of me as she made a motion with her hands and held out a piece of meat. I had just finished eating and they were offering me even more food, WOW! Virginia held onto the string but didn't walk right next to my body as I gingerly took one step at a time towards where Oliva was holding the piece of meat. When I reached her and ate my treat, they both smiled and made heart signs with their hands. Did they love me or love the way I tried to walk on three legs? Were they going to help me look for my leg now? After trying this a few times, they took me back inside to the desk where they had first taken my pictures.

I looked around and saw more signs to try to read, but the sign I liked the most was one that said, "Family Visiting Room." I remembered God telling

me about a special family that he found for me, so I thought they might be in this room. I walked over to the room and looked inside, but I didn't see any people. As my friends helped me walk through the door, I saw that there were couches and chairs and even shelves with treats as well as soft toys for me to toss up in the air with my mouth. Olivia threw a ball my way and I just looked at it and gave it a sniff. It didn't smell like tasty meat, but it was squishy, so I sat down and chomped on it with my teeth. Not tasty, but fun to chew! We played with toys for a while and practiced my sitting skills before going outside so I could smell where other dogs had been and I could leave my scent behind, too. They even let me walk without the string because we were in an enclosed yard where I could play with the other dogs.

Meeting Molly

Many dogs came up to sniff me, but I was afraid and tucked my tail under my belly. One dog that was about my size, but had four legs, sat down next to me, and looked over my way. I could see in her eyes that she had been somewhere that was like The Place of Dirt and that was why she was sad. Olivia and Virginia must have understood that this pup and I were somehow alike, so they took us both back inside to the room with the blankets, couches, snacks, and toys. I was getting tired and the place where my leg used to be began to throb. (I wasn't sure how something that had vanished could still be so painful!) Virginia did her talking again even though she knew that I couldn't hear her, but I could tell my new dog friend could! Her ears perked up and when Olivia showed her a ball, she sat and waited. Olivia threw the ball, and my new friend caught the ball in mid-air; she was talented! (Sitting and catching must be a good thing to do because my dog friend was given a snack right away.) Olivia grabbed another ball off the shelf and showed it to me and waited for me to sit. I tried to do it on my own and realized if I put my front left leg in the center of my body, I could balance better and sit up tall and strong. Once I did this, Olivia tossed me the ball, and I caught it in my mouth just like the other dog. Virginia and Olivia smiled at me and showed me hand-hearts; they were proud!

After playing with the ball, my new dog friend and I laid down in the Family Visiting Room, waiting, I presumed, for this family God had mentioned. We kept waiting, but no one came, and I was sad. In my heart I knew it was because my ears didn't work and that I was missing a leg. Following a short nap, Olivia and Virginia took my new friend and I back outside where I saw that we were the only two dogs in the fenced area. I looked at the other dog and she put her bottom up in the air and wagged her tail; I knew this meant she wanted to play. I did not know if I could play with just three legs but when the other dog pounced my way, I pounced right back and wagged my tail! I looked at Olivia and Virginia and they were both crying; but I could *feel* that they were happy and not sad. I became tired very quickly, so the ladies put a stop to the pouncing and led us back inside.

We walked together (but I mostly hobbled) down the long hallway to the room of crates. Uh-oh, I knew what this meant; they were leaving me alone again for the night. The other dog who had played with me stood by my side looking up at Olivia and Virginia. They shrugged their shoulders and brought my new friend's crate next to mine. I noticed a sign on my friend's crate that I could read, it said, "Dog's Name: Molly, family coming tomorrow for Adoption." It was so nice knowing my friend's name and that she had a family that was coming soon, but when I looked at my crate, all I saw was the blanket and soft toy. I did not have a sign, or a name, or a family.

How could any family want me, a deaf tri-paw with no name? I was so sad and hobbled into my crate and laid on my blanket. Molly was in her crate, and I noticed her lay down as close to the side as she could so we could be near one another. Olivia and Virginia made the hand-heart signs towards me and did the talking mouth motions to Molly. They turned out the lights, and I closed my eyes and whimpered. I felt Molly's paw reach for mine, somehow telling me it would be okay, and then I fell into a dreamless sleep.

The next morning as the sun was coming through the windows, Molly looked over at me with love in her eyes. There was a new sign hanging on her crate that read, "Molly goes home with her family today, please bathe her right away this morning." Olivia and Virginia came in with some clear water and food to fill our bowls. As I was eating and drinking, Olivia took Molly out of her crate and over to a big metal bowl with water coming out of a hose. Olivia couldn't be thinking of giving Molly all that water!

Without warning, I saw her take Molly's long string off her neck and gently take the hose to put water on Molly's fur. I began to bark and make noise, but Virginia came over to me and patted my head and showed me hand-hearts over and over. Molly appeared to be doing okay when they started rubbing bubbles all over her body and I realized this must be the bath she needed before going to the place called home. I stayed with Virginia and thought that if Molly liked this bath idea, good for her, but there was no way they were going to trick me into putting all those bubbles and water on my fur! When the bath was over, Molly shook all the water off her skin and soaked Olivia in the process; that will show her who needs a bath, I thought! After this whole ordeal, Molly came over to stand next to me again and I felt better. I thought that she might take me with her to this home with a family, but first we needed to find my leg.

I was the only one who seemed to want to look for my leg because everyone else wanted me to try to walk and play with just three legs. We went outside together, and I realized that I was walking along without anyone next to my side. Molly must have been happy about this because she started the pouncing game, and I joined in the fun. Olivia and Virginia were full of smiles and showed us many hand-hearts.

After we played and left our scent for the other dogs to know that we had been in the yard, we went inside to the Family Visiting Room. Molly ran all over and I decided to lay down because I was tired from playing the pouncing game. I looked at the couches and realized they looked softer than the toys I would toss in the air or the ones that were lying inside of my crate. I carefully stepped up to one and jumped onto the large, soft cushions. I looked at Olivia and Virginia and they smiled and made the hand-hearts repeatedly. Molly even jumped on the couch and laid down next to me, and just as I thought we would be taking a nap together before resuming the search for my leg, Olivia and Virginia sat down next to us and did their talking with their mouths that I could not hear.

Molly put her paw on mine, and I somehow felt that I would not see her anymore after today. I realized getting off the couch was harder than getting up onto it, so Olivia helped me down as I turned and looked one last time at Molly. Even though I could not hear words, I had a feeling that it was time for Molly to go with her family and it was time for me to leave because I did not have a family. Molly looked sad, and my heart felt like it had formed a big lump in my throat. I hobbled out the door with Olivia while Virginia remained in the room with Molly. I saw a tall man and lady with two small children walk through the door and go towards the Family Visiting Room; they were carrying a circle of material with a dangling shape from it that said "Molly." Molly's family had come for her, and I could only pray that once I found my leg, a family would come for me and take me to live with them forever.

    That night, I was alone again, and I did not even bother to whimper. Molly was gone, Olivia and Virginia only wanted to be with me during the day, and I had not found my leg anywhere that I looked. I had given up on making my ears ever work, but thought that if I at least had my leg, a family would not care about me being deaf. I fell asleep remembering my mom and God promising me in my dream about finding a family and wondered when that would happen. I wanted so much for a family to come to the Family Visiting Room to play with me so that I could show them that I could be the best puppy around, even without a leg or ears that didn't work.

<u>Visitors</u>

When I woke up the next morning to the smell of my bowls being filled with food and clean water, I could *feel* the excitement pouring out of Olivia and Virginia. What was happening? I was surprised to read a sign on my crate that said, "Family background checked for a visit with female deaf tripaw today." I. READ. THAT. AGAIN. Did this mean a family was coming to visit me even though my ears were broken, and I had not found my missing leg? This was happening today?!?

I was getting extremely excited, until I glanced across the room and saw Virginia fill the big metal bowl with water that came from the hose. "Oh no," I thought, "not the bath!" I crouched in the corner of my crate and hoped that Olivia understood that I had no intention of EVER getting wet! She had to get inside the crate with me to try to coax me towards the big metal bowl. I wouldn't move on my own because I was being stubborn, but Olivia just picked me up and carried me across the room. This was the worst; first I learned my ears didn't work unless I was dreaming, then someone stole my leg, and now a bath! God had promised me a family, but there sure seemed to be lots of things that had to happen first!

After the sheer humiliation of my bath, I was rewarded with some more clear water and a nice bowl of food. I then went outside and wondered why Olivia and Virginia were by the fence and not by my sides. They knelt and Olivia had her arm make a big waving motion towards her chest while Virginia held out something that smelled delicious. I looked around and saw no one else to help me, so I tried walking by myself. It was hard and hurt a lot, but I wanted what Virginia had in her hand and I assumed that Olivia wanted me to come towards here because she kept making that same motion over and over. I carefully took one step at a time all by myself, and when I reached my new friends, I was given one tiny piece of meat and lots of hugs and kisses. We then went inside, and I found a new sign on the wall that I could read. It said, "Animals going home today: Gertie and Toby." If a family was coming to visit today, would I get a name and be added to the list? It was all so confusing.

I knew it was important to remember the promise God and my mom had made AND the sign that I read on my crate that said a family WAS visiting the female deaf tri-paw today. A visit must be a good thing for a dog to have with a family. I decided to follow the sign I had read before and go into the Family Visiting Room. Olivia and Virginia followed along and worked with me to sit, stay, and get a treat, which was my favorite part of that game.

Suddenly, I used my nose and detected the scent of two new people getting closer. Was my family here? I looked up and there was a tall man with short hair and a smaller lady with long, curly hair. They were smiling and waving to me as Olivia and Virginia let them into the room. I was so excited that I tried to get to them too fast and fell right over. I was mortified and felt that the new people would never like me now! However, I was wrong; they both came over to me and helped me stand and they each gave me hugs and made heart signs with their hands.

Olivia, Virginia, and the two new people used their talking words that I could not hear, but that was okay because as they were talking, I was able to lay right down between the man and lady and they kept petting me and smiling as they showed me hand-hearts. This had to be good news!

After the four adults finished talking, a very sad thing happened. The people I thought might be my family walked out the door after hugging me goodbye. Had they decided that I wasn't good enough because I couldn't hear and had a missing leg? The lady with the curly hair quickly came back and looked into my eyes and touched her heart and my heart at the same time. She was trying so hard to tell me something, but what? After they left, I just sat on the couch and wouldn't even play with any of the stuffed toys or balls. Olivia and Virginia tried to give me treats, but I wasn't interested.

Then, wonder of all wonders, after only a brief time, my nose detected the scent of the adults again. They were back and standing by the door to the Family Visiting Room, AND they had brought other people! There was another tall young man that resembled the first man I met and standing by him were two younger ladies with curly hair like the woman who touched her heart and mine before she had left earlier. I could tell who these people were; they were all part of the same family...and they were all here together with ME in the Family Visiting Room!

We had such fun; they took turns throwing me the ball and they would hold one end of a rope toy and I would try to tug the other end! They watched me do the sit and stay game and I was glad that they knew the rules and gave me treats when I sat up like a good girl. Everything was going so well, and I didn't even think of my missing leg or that my ears didn't work; but then my heart sank as they started getting ready to leave, and just when I thought they were going to be my family. They all hugged me and made heart signs, and the nice mom touched her heart and mine again, but they still left! I whined, cried, and tried to get to the door, but I fell again, and the mom looked back at me with tears in her eyes.

I couldn't even walk back down the hall to my crate because I was so sad, and I realized that no one wanted me because I WAS a deaf tri-paw. Olivia carried me to my crate while Virginia filled up my water bowl and tried to give me treats. I turned my head away and whimpered sadly. They shut the door and left, and I was all alone. After I was in my crate, I once again read the sign about the family coming to visit, but it didn't matter, nothing mattered, and I cried myself to sleep.

After a long and lonely night, I opened my eyes slowly as I felt the warmth of the sunbeams shining through the windows once again. As I stretched and yawned, I looked up at the side of my crate and saw a new sign to read: "Potential family for female deaf tri-paw bringing family dogs for a visit today." This was good news, the family was coming back AND they were bringing their dogs to visit, too! We would have so much fun, and I could hardly wait, but I did take the time to eat my breakfast and go outside to leave my scent for the other dogs at Sunshine's Sanctuary to find out that I was there. Surely, I would be going to my new home today!

After I ate, Olivia and Virginia stayed outside with me instead of taking me to the Family Visiting Room. I found this strange, but I was happy to lay down on the soft grass and let the sun warm my face. I must have fallen asleep, because when I opened my eyes, I saw some of the same people from yesterday, but this time it was only the ones who I recognized as the parents of the family. They were opening the back of their car and out jumped three dogs! Could all these dogs already be part of this family? I could tell from their scents that two of them were girls and one was a boy, but Olivia and Virginia didn't seem to want me to get near them right away. The three dogs walked around and sniffed the air while eyeing me suspiciously. I wasn't sure they wanted to meet me, but I wanted to meet them and show them that I could be their sister because I was a loving dog.

Olivia and Virginia gave the new dogs lots of meaty treats that I liked to eat, and they walked closer to me, but they began to raise the hair on their backs and show me their teeth. What had I done? Their mom came over to me and made the heart sign with her hands as she kissed the top of my head. Her three dogs were accepting of this and came closer to sniffing the place where my leg used to be as I stood very still. After this, they walked away, and their humans loaded them up into the car. "Don't go," I wanted to say, and I began to whimper again like I had the day before. Once again, the mom with the curly hair came over to me and hugged my neck and kissed my head. Then she touched the place where my leg used to be and made the hand-heart sign as tears streamed down her smiling face. Did this mean she loved me without my leg? Had she realized that my ears didn't work yet? She walked backwards towards her car, waving to me the whole time, and then they were gone.

Will They Come Back?

Why did they keep leaving? Didn't they want me to go to their home? Were they mad that my ears didn't work or did they not like that my leg was missing? That night I decided that I would wake up the next day and look harder for my missing leg to see if that would help the family bring me to their home. When I was sleeping, my mom and God came to me in another dream and my ears once again worked perfectly so I could hear what they were saying. God picked both mom and I up and carried us in His arms to a park bench where we could see other dogs playing with children. Somehow, I realized that God was showing me that this was where my mom now lived with Him in Heaven. Mom put her paw on my heart as God looked at both of us and said, "You two will always be a family, but now your mom wants you to go with this new family that I chose to take care of you on Earth. I will take care of your mom now, and we will both love you forever." I looked at God and replied, "I don't want to leave mom and I don't think this family wants me because they keep leaving." God smiled and hugged us both as He said, "This family must follow certain rules before they can bring you home. It will take time, but you will see that you belong together."

God sat mom near a rainbow that was going through the clouds down to Earth, and she walked over to me and looked in my eyes. I knew she was going to stay with God and that when I woke up, my ears wouldn't work like they did in the dream. I hid my head in God's arms as He petted me and I saw my mom walking farther away from me, towards the other dogs and children in the park. I missed her already and began to cry alone in the crate in the big, dark room.

I awoke to Virginia rubbing my ears and Olivia pouring water into my bowl. They were picking up stuffed toys and balls that were scattered throughout the room. Then they put the long, thick string loosely around my neck and led me outside. When I looked up, I saw them, the family with the three dogs! They had come back! The curly-haired mom and short-haired dad waved at me and showed me hand-hearts. Their young adult children were smiling from ear to ear and each of them also held a long, thick string that was attached to each of the family's dogs. Were we all going to play together? I started to walk over to them, but the dogs began to show me their teeth again! What had I done? I tried to back up and I fell over, but the mom and dad of the dogs and younger people ran right over to my side.

After I stood up with help, and they showed me lots of hand-hearts, they began to walk me over to their children and dogs. The three dogs looked at me suspiciously and they began to shake. I had seen this before at The Place of Dirt when the mean humans would come out and grab onto one of the dog's chains and pull them along behind them, never to be seen again. However, I didn't see any mean people or any chains, so I wasn't sure why they were shaking.

I was able to get a little closer and see that these dogs had circles around their necks with dangling shapes, just like Molly had on her neck. I knew this meant these dogs had names, so I used my reading talents to see that the female dog with long ears and droopy eyes was named "Frances," the fluffy dog went by the name of "Carmella," and the boy dog was called "Ernie." I could only pray that I would be able to have a circle around my neck with a dangling shape soon.

Sadly, I then turned to see them opening the doors to their car, and I knew that meant they were all going to get in and drive off again. I was so sad that I collapsed in the grass and watched them go as they waved to me out the window. Is this what God had meant about following the rules; they had to leave every day and could only be my family part of the time? Olivia and Virginia could see that I was depressed, and they tried to get me to play. I wanted to show them that I was an obedient dog, so I caught the ball in my mouth and chewed on it a bit before I went back into Sunshine's Sanctuary.

I knew what would happen now; they would put me in the crate with a stuffed toy and blanket. They would then shut off the lights and close the door and disappear until the next morning. I didn't like it, but I was a deaf tri-paw and had nowhere else to go. That night, I couldn't sleep well and realized that I had not had time to look for my leg, but I was also able to eat, drink, play, and run without it being attached to my body. I thought about only being able to hear in my dreams and began to wonder if just possibly *having* ears was enough. Did the family who visited me only come during the day and then leave again because I could not hear and I was missing a leg, or was it just because of the rules that God told me about in my dream? I was determined to believe God's promise to me about the family and I also began to realize that even though my dog-mom was in Heaven, I could still love her, and I would always be her little pup.

For the next several weeks, the family of five with three dogs would visit for a brief time during the day and then they would leave. They would take turns feeding me tasty treats and even brought me toys, which I would share with the other dogs at

Sunshine's Sanctuary. Sometimes during these visits, their dogs would snarl at me, and sometimes they wouldn't even look at me and I believed it was because I was different. I realized that they were their own pack, but I wanted to be part of their pack very badly and prayed each night that the next day would be the day when I could go home instead of just visiting with the people and their dogs.

<u>Finally...a Family to Call my Own</u>

I awoke on a very sunny day in late July and read a new sign on my crate, "Female Deaf Tri-Paw to go home today." WHAT WAS THIS WONDERFUL NEWS? Could it be true? Was the family God had promised me in both of my dreams *really* taking me to their home today? I stood up in my crate while Olivia and Virginia were getting the hose ready to fill the big metal bowl with water, and I just knew that meant I would have to get wet and full of soap bubbles, but I didn't care if it meant my very own family was waiting for me to live with them forever!

I slowly ate my breakfast because I had learned how to be a dog with good manners, and I drank some of the clear water from the bowl in the crate before hobbling over for my bath. Olivia and Virginia were all smiles, and while I couldn't hear their words, I could *feel* their excitement in my heart. After the degrading experience of water and bubbles being all over me, they dried me off and took me for a walk outside. I looked around for the car that usually brought my family for a visit, but I didn't see it anywhere! Had they forgotten to come, or worse yet changed their minds because I WAS a deaf tri-paw?

We went back inside, and Olivia walked me into the Family Visiting Room while Virginia went to the desk by the door to get some papers. Before I knew what was happening, my nose sniffed the scent of the people who had been coming every day for a month to visit me at Sunshine's Sanctuary; they were here! I looked at the door and in walked the dad, mom, and their oldest daughter. The other two family members and the three dogs were not with them, and I wondered if they were outside looking for my lost leg. I could see that the mom had something hiding in her hands and I could not tell what it was, so I sat like a good girl and waited to see if it was a treat for me to chomp.

I was receiving lots of pats on the head and shown hand-hearts from the three people whom I hoped were my family. Virginia was showing the papers she had taken from the desk to them, and the mom took a sort of stick (it smelled like plastic) to scribble words on the papers; there sure were a lot of them and it took a long time. Olivia gave the people a bag of small pieces of food that were like the ones from the bowl in my crate, along with a fluffy bed and a stuffed toy. All three of the people were smiling, and I hoped that they didn't think food, a fluffy bed, and a toy were better than a dog like me, even though my ears didn't work, and my leg seemed to have disappeared forever.

The mom of the group gave Olivia her phone and then the family made big arm motions towards me that I knew meant I was supposed to come to where they were sitting. I gently walked over to them and sat down. Virginia was waving her arms at me and making hand-hearts, so I looked right at her as Olivia pointed the phone our way and took photos. (What was it with humans and pictures anyhow?)

I could not believe what happened next as the lady knelt next to me and showed me what was in her hand; it was a neck circle with a dangling shape! She was crying as she hugged and kissed me and showed me what the dangling shape said. I saw her lips move and figured she didn't know about my reading talents yet, but I read along anyhow since I couldn't hear her words. I saw the most beautiful words in my life, "I am deaf. My name is Gennie Marie, and I am friendly. Call my family." I put my head on the lady's shoulder because I now knew that she was my new mom, and we just sat there together as the rest of the people in the room used their mouths to say words. I felt in my heart a love that I had not felt since the last day I saw my dog-mom in The Place of Dirt.

Olivia and Virginia walked us out of Sunshine's Sanctuary, and I somehow knew that I wouldn't see them ever again. My new sister helped me get in the backseat of the car and sat right next to me as my new mom and dad hopped in the front seat. Olivia and Virginia came to where I was sitting and gave me hugs and kisses. They showed me hand-hearts repeatedly and I gave each of them a kiss with my tongue.

I began to see that from the time I was rescued from The Place of Dirt until this very day, God had given me many helpers. First, there was Trudy and her team of people from Rosie's Rescue who took all of us away from the abuse and torture we went through down south where the tractor had run me over and left me for dead. Then I had met Tommy at Salvadore's Animal Hospital and realized he had helped me get healthy and never left me alone. Wilbur was the one who drove me all the way to Sunshine's Sanctuary where I met Olivia and Virginia and I was able to learn how to be a clever dog by following the example of my friend, Molly. Finally, I had met the people whom God had chosen to be my family and I was going home.

As I was thinking about everything that had happened, Olivia shut the car door and she and Virginia backed away from the car. This was IT; what God promised was happening! Everyone waved and I stuck my head out the window to feel the breeze on my face as I headed home with my family.

Home

    My new dad didn't have to drive far until we reached the street where I would live. I knew when we were home because the other two young adult children of the family and the three dogs were all standing outside. Everyone was waving at me and showing me hand-hearts while the dogs ran around in excitement. After parking, dad helped me get out and I sniffed the air; I could smell the scent of my new family everywhere!

    I looked over and saw a large yard where I could play. My curly-haired sisters and tall brother opened a gate for me to go into the yard to play with my dog-siblings. I remembered their names from reading the dangling shapes on their neck circles and I figured they would want to read my name too, so they knew that I was Gennie Marie, their sister. I stood perfectly still, which is always hard to do when balancing on only three legs. Frances, Carmella, and Ernie sniffed me all over because they were getting to know me better. I did not want them to snarl or show me their teeth again, so I sat and was a good girl. After a while, they walked away, and I explored the yard. I could smell the three dogs everywhere and I left my scent behind so they would know I was going to live with them now.

I began to get tired and that was when I laid down to rest. However, I became extremely nervous because I saw something very strange that I had only seen a long time ago outside the door of the old rickety house at The Place of Dirt; my new family had steps going into their home. What was I going to do now? I could barely walk on the flat ground without stumbling, let alone go up steps! My new mom saw me looking at the steps and came over and gave me a big hug while putting the long, thick string around my neck. Dad was on one side of me, and my brother was on the other side. Mom gently led me along with the string, but I stopped as soon as we were at the bottom of the steps. My sisters walked up and down them several times while smiling at me, but I would not budge; then Frances, Carmella, and Ernie went up the steps and into the house.

Was this the only way inside? Everyone took a turn showing me how the stairs worked for them, but I was afraid, and not just of the steps. I was afraid that if I fell, these people would not want me anymore. What if I could not make it up the steps?

Surprisingly, my new family was very patient and decided to sit down on the ground next to me and wait. As we waited, I rested my head in my mom's lap, and everyone took turns petting me as the sun shone down on what had become an extremely sweltering day. I wondered if it might be cooler inside the house, so I gradually stood up and everyone looked at me encouragingly. Once again, my new brother was on one side, and my dad was on my other side; mom took the long, thick string and gently led me up to the door one step at a time. My sisters were at the top step clapping and showing me hand-hearts. I had made it inside!!!

Once we were all in the house, I began sniffing everywhere, but I had to lay down because I was so tired from the exciting day and finally being able to go home with my family. As I was laying down, my new dog-siblings came over again to sniff me, but I was too tired to play. They showed me their teeth a little bit, but not as much as before so I hoped that meant they were happy with me becoming their sister. I fell asleep for what must have been a long time because when I opened my eyes it was dark outside.

Suddenly, waves of a wonderful scent came my way; it was meat! My sisters were ready to help me walk to a room that smelled like various kinds of food, so I knew we were in the kitchen. My brother was making sure all the dogs were sitting patiently waiting for their meals while mom and dad were filling four bowls with the delicious-smelling tiny pieces of meat. This wasn't like the dry bits of food that Olivia and Virginia gave me, but it was like the tiny treats Trudy had first given me at The Place of Dirt when she rescued me and the other dogs. The only difference was, there were lots of bites of meat AND even blueberries and vegetables. The scent of the food wasn't like anything I had ever smelled before, and I could hardly wait to eat it all! I also noticed bowls of clear water in different spots in the kitchen and knew that this meant I could have clean, cold water whenever I needed a drink. This place was nothing like The Place of Dirt and I loved it already!

Once mom and dad sat all our bowls of food down, I decided to try everyone's meal, but this was not a clever idea and not a good way to try to become friends with the other dogs. They snarled and bared their teeth like never before and all five of my humans immediately separated us as they looked at me very sternly and made a motion with their first two fingers tapping their thumbs. I knew right away this meant "no," so I tried to be good again and sit down, but instead I slid all the way down onto the floor.

Sadly, my first dinner with my family didn't go very well. After Frances, Carmella, and Ernie ate their food, my dad helped me get back up and showed me where my food bowl would be and that everyone was supposed to eat in their own spot. I slowly ate the most delicious meal I had ever tasted, and I couldn't believe the other dogs weren't trying to take it away! Did this mean we weren't supposed to fight for food like dogs used to do at The Place of Dirt?

After dinner, everyone went into a spacious room with furniture. My family even had steps up to the couches and chairs to make it easier for me and the other dogs to be able to get up and down. These steps weren't hard like the outside ones but seemed to be more like a firm pillow. I sniffed them and decided I would think about trying them out later. I saw stuffed toys and balls to play with and my brother looked like he wanted to throw me a ball, so I sat down and waited patiently, just like Molly used to do at Sunshine's Sanctuary. Sure enough, he threw the ball to me, and I caught it in my mouth. Everyone smiled and clapped their hands together! Then the other dogs wanted to play, but they didn't seem to want to share the ball or their family with me because they looked my way with a warning snarl. I decided that they needed to adjust to me being in their family and that maybe I would just go to bed.

Suddenly, I spotted ANOTHER set of stairs, only this time there were many more of them to climb. In fact, there were so many steps that I couldn't see all the way to the top! I looked at the other dogs and they ran right up the stairway without a second thought to my problem. Dad started to lift me to carry me upstairs, but I wanted to try; ever so slowly I put my left front leg on the steps and waited. Then I brought up my back legs and tried for the next step, and the next, and the next! After an exceptionally long time, I finally made it to the top where there was a big hallway. Everyone was smiling and they each came over to give me a hug; I had climbed the steps all by myself! I was even more surprised than my new family at this new step-climbing ability!

Everyone began going into different rooms and I wasn't sure what I was supposed to do until mom stuck her head out of one of the doors and made that big motion with her arm moving towards her chest that I knew meant "come." I hobbled along to this new room where mom and dad were, and I saw the biggest bed ever! This wasn't your regular kind of dog bed; it was a bed that was standing on wooden legs and must be for humans! I began to sit down on the floor when, to my astonishment, mom showed me another set of steps that led right up to the bed. Was she serious, more steps? I was very tired at this point, but I saw my new dog-siblings going right up the steps to lay on the bed like that was where they belonged. Did my new family really allow dogs in their bed all night long?

I looked again at the steps and just wasn't sure, so dad came over and picked me up and placed me gently on the bed before he and mom got into bed with me, Frances, Carmella, and Ernie; four dogs and two people in one bed...unbelievable! Mom kissed the other dogs and then pointed to my dangling shape that I knew said my name, Gennie Marie, and that I was deaf and friendly. She put her right hand on my heart and her left hand on her own heart before kissing me goodnight. Was she telling me that she loved me in a way that I could hear even though my ears didn't work? It did not take me long to fall asleep in my new home with my family next to me in the giant bed.

My New Life and My New Cousin

    I woke up the next day and saw mom smiling as she reached out to each of us and smiled as she gave us a kiss. Dad was already gone, and I could tell mom was trying to get ready for something. Frances, Carmella, and Ernie used the steps to get off the bed, but I still wasn't sure about them so I saw mom look down the hallway and open her mouth to use words I couldn't hear once again. In came my brother and the shortest sister in our family; they were ready to help. The three of them guided me down the bed-steps and I was surprised that it was easier than I thought. Two of my human siblings went downstairs with the other dogs, but I wanted to wait for mom. She went into a small room with clothes hanging on racks and reached up to grab a shirt and pants.

After she changed, we walked through the hall together to the top of the steps. She looked at me and did a hand-heart and I just *knew* that she wanted me to walk down those steps. Going up was one thing, but going down meant I could tumble all the way to the bottom of the stairs! Mom sat on the top step with me and waited patiently. I was less afraid when she was by my side, so I decided to try my best. The only leg I had in the front went down first, followed by the back two, again and again until I was almost galloping. I was faster than I thought! When I arrived at the last step, I was already tired, but I could smell the scent of the meat, fruit, and vegetables coming from the kitchen, so I decided to go in that direction. I couldn't believe my eyes; there was more fresh water AND my very own bowl was again full of more yummy food for breakfast. I remembered what happened the night before at dinner, so I took my time eating and tried hard to ignore the other dogs who were eating out of their dishes.

After breakfast, mom walked into a different room of the house that had a computer on a desk. I also saw books and papers in folders. She sat down and typed words on the keyboard when suddenly another face appeared on the screen. I read the word "Zoom" in the corner of the screen and realized that my mom was talking with this young girl right through the screen; it was amazing! Even though I couldn't hear what they were saying, I knew that mom was helping the little girl learn because she used her books and papers while talking to the person who was inside the screen. How did someone live inside of a computer anyhow? I decided this was more than I could figure out at the time, so I looked for my siblings.

My brother was letting the other dogs outside and I decided I would try going down the steps to the yard. Sure enough, it worked just like it did with the inside stairs, and I made it to the bottom by taking my time and going slowly. Once I was in the yard, my brother started throwing balls to each of us and I knew this meant it was playtime! I noticed that Ernie wanted to chase them, but Frances and Carmella let the balls go right past their heads. That was fine with me because I would be happy to play ball and when my human brother saw this, he kept tossing the balls to me and I would get them in my mouth and chomp them for a while.

Before too long, a car appeared in the driveway and out came my oldest sister with a big female dog! Where did she find that dog? The dog came right into our yard, and I could tell that Frances, Carmella, and Ernie were not happy about it one bit! However, this new dog came right over to me and began quietly sniffing where my leg used to be, and I saw that she also had a neck circle with a dangling shape. I knew that this meant my oldest sister was this dog's mom and I could tell how much she loved her because she kept smiling the biggest smile whenever she looked over at the dog whose name was Luna.

After Luna finished smelling where my left leg used to be, she walked around the yard. My new sibling-dogs stood their ground and barked at Luna. I was sure glad I couldn't hear them because they were barking a lot, and I could tell my human siblings wanted them to stop. Luna put her nose to the ground everywhere in the yard and left her scent behind so my family would know that she had visited. She kept glancing my way as if she was trying to figure out why I was there. I wondered if she was trying to find my leg when she suddenly came over and put her head down towards the ground with her bottom in the air and her tail wagging; she wanted to play! No dog had wanted to play with me since I met my friend Molly back at Sunshine's Sanctuary and I was so excited! I tried to slowly walk over to my brother to see if he would throw the ball to me and Luna. Even though Luna was bigger than me, she never once tried to hurt me, and we played "catch the ball" with my brother while the other dogs decided to ignore us and laid down under the shade tree.

We played until our tongues were hanging out of our mouths and I became very tired. The sun was getting hotter, and I saw mom come outside and do the big hand motion that I knew meant she wanted me to come to where she was standing. All the dogs ran over to her with me following behind as carefully as possible. I knew I would have to walk up the steps again to get inside, but this time I didn't need any help; I did it all by myself! My humans were so excited that they showed me hand-hearts and clapped their hands repeatedly.

Once we were inside, I could smell food that was on the table; was it time to eat again? Should I try to jump up to get the food off the table since it wasn't in my food bowl? As soon as I tried to jump towards the table, mom showed me the no sign by putting her thumb and first two fingers together and making a very angry face; I didn't want to make mom mad, so I laid down like a good girl. My family sat down to eat at the table while the other dogs and I sat on the cool floor nearby in case any food would happen to come our way.

After everyone finished eating, mom went back to her desk to turn on her computer and a new person's face popped up for me to see. Did that mean two people lived inside the screen? It was so confusing to me until I read a folder that was in mom's desk drawer that said, "Tutor Files," and that was when I learned my mom was a tutor and could work right from this desk in my new home. I decided to lay down on the big cushion mom had right next to her desk when I noticed Carmella walk into the room. This was the first time one of my dog-siblings approached me on their own and I was hoping that meant we could be friends. Carmella looked at mom and my mom picked her up and showed her to the boy who lived inside the computer screen. He smiled and waved so I thought he would want to meet me, too. I tried to get up to the screen and mom smiled and helped me stand as she moved her mouth and said something to her student. He smiled, waved, and made hand-hearts. I was incredibly happy that I was being a helpful dog by being part of mom's work, but I was tired and laid down again while Carmella looked at me suspiciously. Mom kept talking to her student and showing him something in a book when I suddenly felt Carmella's furry little body lie down next to me and we both fell happily asleep.

When I woke up, mom was not by the computer anymore, so I went on a search for my family. They were all sitting in the spacious room where the chairs, couches, and dog toys were located. Luna and my oldest sister were still there, and I was glad to see that Frances and Ernie didn't snarl at me when I walked into the room. I saw that dad was back home and sitting in one of the chairs, so I went over to give him a big kiss with my tongue since he hadn't seen me in a while. He laughed and showed me hand-hearts while the other dogs all came over for some attention from dad as well. After my oldest sister and Luna left, I could smell the scent of the food that I recognized as my breakfast and dinner. I walked into the kitchen and saw my youngest sister pour some more clear water into our dishes and remembered that I would have to be incredibly good and mindful of not eating out of the food bowls that belonged to Frances, Carmella, and Ernie.

That night, I knew that I would need to walk up the stairs to get to the place where I would be able to sleep in the giant bed. I remembered how I had done it before and I was determined to do it again, and this time I was even a bit stronger and steadier than before! I made it to the top with everyone else and received hugs and kisses from mom, dad, my brother, and my sister. I even used the soft bed-steps on my own and waited for my new parents to kiss us all goodnight. I fell asleep telling myself that even though it was taking my new dog-siblings time to adjust to me, we could still be a family and that I would do everything I could to be their friend.

The Dreaded Paw-dicure and a Trip to the Store

After living with my family for a few weeks, I woke up on what I knew was a weekend because no one was rushing to begin their workday and dad was still at home. Frances, Carmella, Ernie, and I ate our breakfast, and I didn't even need to be reminded not to eat from their bowls anymore. My oldest sister brought Luna over and I was sure it was time for another play date with my cousin who was quickly becoming my best friend.

As Luna and I were wrestling over a stick, and she decided to try to play Keep Away, I looked through the fence and saw a strange car pull into our driveway. Two ladies I had never seen before got out of the car and began to walk towards the fence. Luna was busy playing with the stick that I let her have and I decided that meant I had to protect the yard! I began growling and showing my teeth as I made the hair on my back stand up on end. Dad quickly ran out of the house and showed me the "no" sign and smiled at the ladies. They waved at him, and dad made words with his mouth that I couldn't hear, but I figured if dad was nice to them that I should sit down to better assess the situation while still being on guard. He let the ladies in the gate and my oldest sister came out of the house and stood near Luna. The ladies showed me hand-hearts, but I still wasn't impressed, and I looked at them very seriously so that they knew that they had better be good humans.

Since Luna had left the stick behind when her mom came outside, I picked it up and took it to the other end of the yard in case the new ladies thought they may want to keep it for themselves. While I kept an eye on what they were doing, the taller one began to empty the big bag she was carrying. I could smell treats, but I was afraid it might be a trick so I stayed with the stick and waited to see what Luna would do first.

Suddenly, the shorter lady took a shiny object in her hand and moved towards Luna's feet. WHAT WAS SHE DOING?? Luna tried to back up, but my oldest sister and my dad held her in place. Then the shorter lady gave Luna some treats to try to make her remain still. Were they going to take off her leg just like the people did to me at Salvadore's Animal Hospital? I wanted to tell Luna to not let these people fool her with treats and I couldn't understand how my dad and sister thought it would be okay to take Luna's leg away!

I began to bark and that was when I saw mom coming out of the back door. She brought me the tasty blueberries that she gave Frances, Carmella, Ernie, and I for snacks. As she sat down next to me and I ate a few berries, I began to wonder why she (of all people) would let these strange people come into our yard to take away Luna's leg. I began to whimper as she petted my head and showed me hand-hearts. I was NOT okay with my family allowing such madness! When I looked at Luna, I was shocked to see she was still eating the treats from the tall lady while the shorter one still had the shiny tool in use around Luna's feet.

Just then, my brother and youngest sister brought out the rest of the dogs. "No," I barked, "go back inside." They must have known what I meant because they tried to turn around and go back through the door, but it was closed. I saw that both ladies had moved away from Luna and that my oldest sister was giving her kisses. I couldn't even begin to look to see what leg they had taken from her when she quickly shook herself off and came running to me...with all four legs thankfully still attached! What kind of trick was this anyhow? I decided that there was no way that I was going to let them take the shiny tool on the only three legs I had left just because they had spared all of Luna's legs.

One after another, the rest of the dogs became duped into smelling the treats and having the shiny tool put on their feet. I closed my eyes and whimpered loudly in fear while mom just kept petting me and putting her right hand on her heart and her left hand on my heart. How could she try to say she loved me when she was letting these people try to take away my dog-siblings' legs? First it was Frances' turn and she laid down and ate their treats, but she was shaking all over and her hair was flying off in every direction. She didn't like this one bit, and even though she had four legs attached to her when they finished, she was still shaking. Next was Carmella and she was panting so hard that I thought her tongue might fall right out of her mouth, but she too had four legs at the end as well! I knew that Ernie would stand his ground because he was a boisterous little dog, but that didn't stop them from using that shiny tool on his feet, too!

I had news for them; I would not comply or let anyone come anywhere near my feet or legs!

What had started as a nice weekend morning was becoming a nightmare in my mind. I tried to make myself as small as possible, but my dad walked right over and picked me up in his arms. The rest of the dogs were eating the blueberries that my brother and sisters gave them, and they seemed fine, but I wasn't sure I would be okay with that shiny tool scaring me so much!

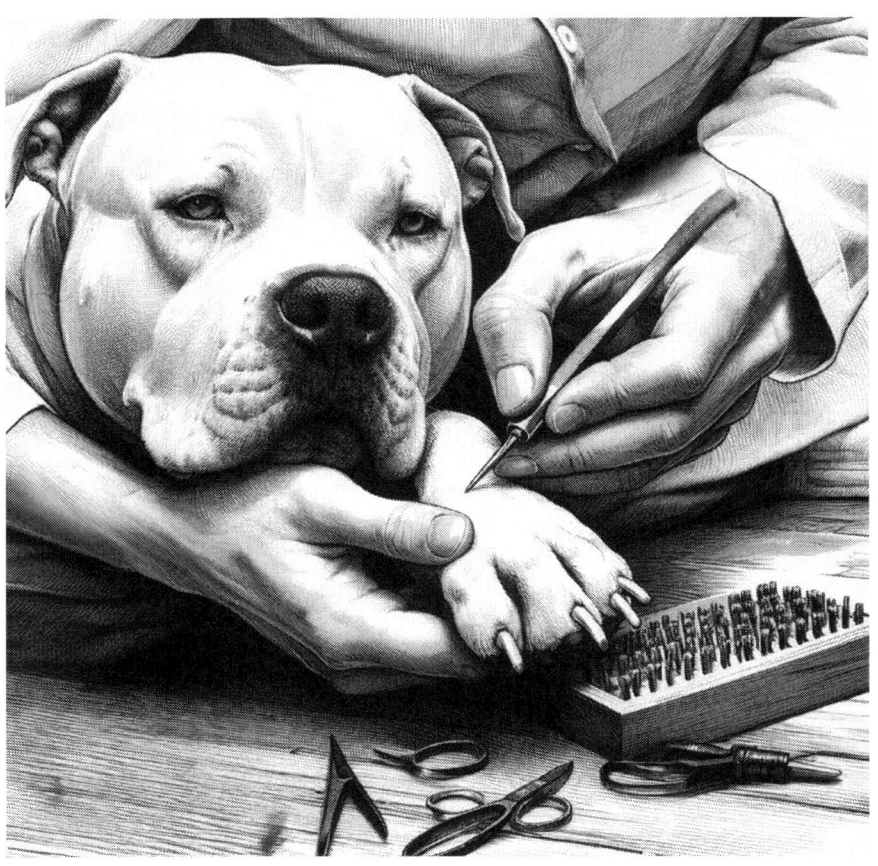

The ladies tried to comfort me by petting me and offering me treats, but I was afraid that they might make me sleepy and when I woke up, one of my other legs would be missing. Mom came over and looked right into my eyes and I could feel her trying to tell me she would never let anyone hurt me again. She gave me three treats from the lady's bag, and she kept petting my head lovingly. As I squeezed my eyes tightly shut, I felt something touch the only front leg I had, and I wondered if mom and dad being near me would make everything okay.

After what seemed like an exceptionally long time, the ladies backed away and dad sat me down in the grass. I was afraid to look at myself, but when I did, I saw that I did indeed have three legs still attached to my body! Thank God Luna, Frances, Carmella, Ernie, and I still had the same number of legs we had started out with that morning! I was so thankful that I went over to the ladies and gave them a kiss with my big tongue. I wanted to let them know that they could come to our yard anytime, but they needed to bring treats!

After everyone's paw-dicure, we all played in the yard together for a while before my oldest sister and Luna went back to their house. Dad came out of the house with the long, thick string and placed it around my neck while mom let the rest of the dogs inside and came back out the door. She opened the gate that led outside our yard and walked out with dad and I following. I didn't know what to think, but I was a little nervous because I wasn't sure if we were walking somewhere or going for a ride.

As we walked closer to the car, dad opened the door for me and helped me get inside. Once we were all buckled in our seats safely, dad started the engine and off we went. I wasn't sure where we were going, but I realized that if I could trust my family during what ended up being a toenail trim, I could trust them with anything. As dad drove out of our driveway, I became so worn out from the morning's adventures that I went to sleep right there in the car.

I woke up from my short nap when I realized that the engine was off because I didn't feel the vibrations anymore. Mom got out of our car and walked over to my side while dad carefully helped me down because it was a little tricky to get out correctly with the seat, the car door, and just having three legs. I noticed many other vehicles and people walking around so I knew that we were in a parking lot. I sat down between my parents and waited to see what to do next. With dad taking the long, thick string on one side of me, and mom on my other side, we began to walk towards a building with doors that slid open and closed each time a person got too close. I saw that there was a large sign over the door which made me realize how handy my reading skills were in life. This had to be the place for me because the letters on the sign spelled out, "Dog Daze." Once inside, I saw toys and bones, food and treats, and shelves of neck circles and everything else a dog would ever need; my parents had taken me to a dog store! I couldn't believe my eyes as we walked up and down the aisles and mom put things into a big metal basket on wheels.

People kept stopping us and saying words to my parents that I could not hear, but I figured that they wanted to pet me because my dad would make me sit nicely and mom would nod her head to the people and show me hand-hearts. I couldn't believe how many people of all ages wanted to take time to see me, Gennie Marie, a friendly, deaf tri-paw. I was a good girl and very patient with all the people as my mom and dad would smile and say words that, even though I could not hear, I knew were words about me being part of their family.

After mom had found everything that we needed, and even extra toys we didn't need, she pushed the big metal basket on wheels up to a lady who was touching buttons on a small machine that was sitting on a long counter. We had to wait in line behind a couple who were buying food for their dog. When the couple looked back and saw me, they took everything that my parents had in our cart and put it on the long counter. My mom began to shake her head no while my dad was opening and closing his mouth and trying to take the items back. I didn't understand what was happening, but the couple looked at the lady behind the small machine and nodded their heads as if to tell her they wanted what was in our cart.

Why couldn't they get their own things from the store to go with their dog's food? I looked at mom and saw that she was crying but smiling at the same time. The couple came over and patted my head while I was being a good girl and staying next to dad. Then they gave mom back everything that was in our cart, and I realized that this kind couple had just bought what my parents were planning to buy for me and my dog-siblings as a gift to my family. At that moment, I began to realize that there were many people with giving hearts in the world and I had been blessed to have met some of these compassionate individuals who had helped me along the way.

<u>Learning How to be Part of a Family</u>

    Over the next several months, I learned that the reason dad was gone for part of the day was because he didn't work from home like mom and my brother. The youngest sister in our family seemed to do a lot of work around a big piece of furniture that she would use by pressing her fingers onto keys and she also worked with something she put up to her mouth and blew air into; I could tell these things made sounds because I felt the vibrations. She also studied books and took notes while looking at her computer, so I guessed she was taking classes over the screen and that her teachers lived inside the computer just like mom's students. I began to understand that my oldest sister and Luna must have their own home because they would come to visit often but didn't sleep in any of the rooms upstairs, except when it was a special holiday. I was the only dog in the family who wanted to play with Luna, and I found that each time she visited, I began to be able to run with her more often in the yard until we both became so tired, we would begin to pant and would lay down together to sleep.

The female fluffy dog, Carmella, would come to lay down next to me in a chair, but when I would try to flip her over like a pancake, she would quiver and run to our mom for help. Mom would make the no sign with her thumb and fingers and look at me with the same face she did when I did something I shouldn't, so I tried to not play the Pancake Game with Carmella, but I wasn't very successful and figured she would like it if I tried often enough. Frances, the female dog with long ears, and Ernie, the short male dog, still stayed away and I began to understand that Frances simply was a lot older than me, and I could tell that she didn't feel like a new puppy, and she preferred to rest, take slow walks, and lay in the sun. Ernie seemed to just want to be in charge and, even though I couldn't hear his bark, I could see that he did it whenever I was near. However, whenever our family would catch the four of us playing with toys or laying together, they would make hand-hearts and smile, so I knew they were happy.

There were lots of people who would come over to meet me and play with Frances, Carmella, and Ernie. Everyone seemed to love to talk to my family and I could tell that they already knew the other dogs. When they met me, I would shyly hobble over and show them my neck circle with the dangling shape so they could read that I was Gennie Marie, and I was a friendly, deaf tri-paw. My favorite visitors were four adults that I figured out were my grandparents, my oldest sister, Luna the dog, a guy who I was told would soon be my newest brother, and a little boy mom took care of and loved.

Whenever the little boy came over, there were these little blocks all over the place that he would use to build things. I tried to eat one once and the little boy looked at my mom in surprise; she showed me the no sign and I dropped it because it didn't taste that good anyhow. There were others who would stop to get to know me, and I always tried to be a loving dog, but I would get so excited and instead I would jump to say hello. Mom and dad would get that stern look on their faces and gently pull me into a seated position. I guess the people I met didn't think jumping was what an obedient dog should do so I tried to stop, but it was hard to be so excited and sit still.

I began to learn that there were times to eat and times to play. I loved it when my family played with me, and I would give them kisses and rest my head on their shoulders as my way of saying I loved them very much. I tried to be quiet when my family was doing their work, but sometimes I just wanted to be a playful puppy. I liked it when mom would show her students who lived in the computer screen that I was there because they would always smile, wave, and show me hand-hearts. Since my ears didn't work, I always wanted to be right next to one of the people in my family so I would know what was happening. Sometimes, the place where my front right leg used to be would hurt and I would limp. Mom or my sister would get out some sort of bag that came from the rectangle that kept food cold and they would place it where my leg used to be and lovingly pet my head as I would quietly fall asleep.

I finally understood that God had been right all those many months ago when He and my first mom spoke to me in a dream. He stayed with me in my scariest moments and showed me that He was taking care of my dog-mom in Heaven. He sent many caring people into my life, and even though I was afraid of them at first because of the cruel humans at The Place of Dirt, He made sure that I was taken care of by these compassionate and animal-

loving individuals until the time came for me to meet my forever family. God made sure I ended up in the exact place He needed me to be, with a family who wanted me and loved me with their whole hearts. As I looked at the people and dogs in my family, I knew that I would never have to worry about my broken ears or look for my missing leg ever again, because I was home, I was part of a family, and I was loved.

About the Author

Tammy Pusateri Puckrin lives with her family near the shores of Lake Erie. She stands strong in her faith, loves to volunteer, and is proud of her Italian heritage. She is a wife and the mother of three amazing human children and four adorable canine children, with many other precious fur babies waiting at the Rainbow Bridge. Tammy is an Author, Executive Assistant for their family businesses, and a Private Tutor. She is the former recipient of the Terrific Teacher Award, 4-H Rookie Volunteer Award, and the Ohio State University Innovator Award. When not writing, Tammy enjoys cross stitching, reading, and scrapbooking. She would love to hear from you on social media or at www.pusateripublications.com

@pusateripublications